Before They Were Famous

Ben Franklin

Written by Stephen Krensky
Illustrated by Bobbie Houser

A Crabtree Crown Book

CRABTREE
Publishing Company
www.crabtreebooks.com

School-to-Home Support for Caregivers and Teachers

This appealing book is designed to teach students about core subject areas. Students will build upon what they already know about the subject, and engage in topics that they want to learn more about. Here are a few guiding questions to help readers build their comprehension skills. Possible answers appear here in red.

Before Reading:

What do I know about this topic?

- *I know that Ben Franklin was a highly intelligent person who invented many useful things.*
- *I know that Ben Franklin signed the Constitution of the United States.*

What do I want to learn about this topic?

- *I want to learn more about Ben Franklin when he was a boy growing up.*
- *I want to know what some of Ben Franklin's inventions were.*

During Reading:

I'm curious to know...

- *I'm curious to learn why Ben Franklin left school when he was ten years old.*
- *I'm curious to learn why the only way Ben could be published was to use a fake name and write letters that were widely talked about.*

How is this like something I already know?

- *I've heard that some authors use a pen name instead of their real name when they write certain articles or stories.*
- *I know that some people have had to leave school to help out in the family business.*

After Reading:

What was the author trying to teach me?

- *I think the author is teaching me that even if you do something well not everyone will appreciate your efforts.*
- *He's teaching me that one should hold on to their dreams and never give up.*

How did the photographs and captions help me understand more?

- *The photos and drawings helped me to imagine how life was during the early 1700s.*
- *The captions made me appreciate how hard it is to succeed when you are a young person.*

Table of Contents

Ben Gets His Start

Young Ben Franklin wasn't happy. He wasn't happy at all. He didn't mind being twelve years old. Twelve was a very grown-up age, he thought.

Fun Facts

Ben was part of a big family. His father, Josiah, had seven children with his first wife. After she died, he had ten more children with his second wife, Abiah. Ben was their eighth child, born in 1706.

And Ben was glad to live in Boston. It was the biggest city in the American **colonies**. The year was 1718, and Boston was growing fast. There were lots of opportunities for someone with a good head on his shoulders.

Ben was sure he had one of those.

BOSTON

Grover
East Boston
Winthrop
BOSTON
Fort Winthrop
Boston Harbor
South Boston
Castle Island
Fort Independence
Old Harbor
Spectacle

He was also relieved to no longer be working for his father. Josiah Franklin made soap and candles for a living. After leaving school at the age of ten, Ben had spent two years cutting wicks, filling dipping **molds**, and serving customers twelve hours a day, six days a week.

Fun Facts

It was common in the Franklin family for younger sons to apprentice to older ones.

The worst part had been the terrible smell from the **vats**. They were filled with tallow, which was the fat from animals used to make soap and candles. The tallow smell was so bad it made you sorry you ever had to breathe.

Stuck in Place

So why was Ben so unhappy? Well, Ben had left his father's trade to become a printer's **apprentice** for his brother, James. Printers printed books and newspapers and advertisements. It was a world filled with reading and writing.

What could be better?

Ben had expected to work with words all day. But he soon discovered that this wasn't what James had in mind. James only wanted Ben to run errands and sweep the floor.

Fun Facts

An apprentice could go to jail if he broke the contract he agreed to with his master.

Over the next four years, very little changed—except that Ben got good at sweeping. True, he had been able to publish two poems. One was about a lighthouse keeper and his family who died in a storm.

The other poem told of the fearsome pirate Blackbeard battling with the British navy.

Fun Facts

Blackbeard's real name was Edward Teach, but that wasn't a scary enough name for a pirate.

But Ben was itching to write more. Sadly, James did not care about Ben's itches. He refused to let Ben write for his newspaper, the *New-England Courant*. He told Ben to be patient. His printing apprenticeship would be done in a few more years.

Ben hated being reminded of that.

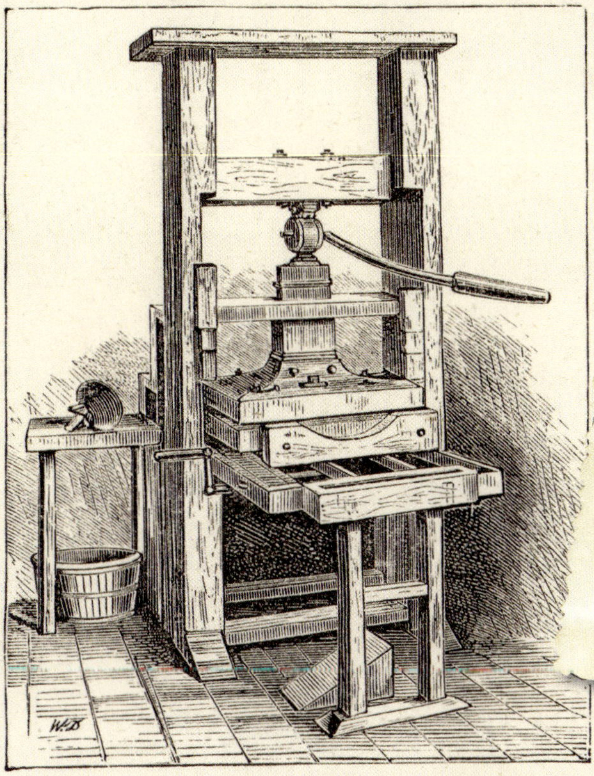

BENJAMIN FRANKLIN'S PRINTING PRESS, 1785.

Fun Facts

In Ben's day, printing presses had barely changed at all in the 250 years since they were first invented.

A modern printing press

A New Contributor

Soon, the *Courant* had a new contributor secretly leaving letters at its door. Her name, she said, was Silence Dogood. She claimed to be a middle-aged widow who was "an enemy to **vice** and a friend to **virtue**." Most importantly, she liked to speak her mind.

The *Courant* and its editor were delighted. Silence Dogood made fun of women's **petticoats**. She also did not approve of people who said they were religious but weren't very nice.

Her letters were widely talked about around town. And everyone was asking the same question. Who was Silence Dogood really? No one seemed to know.

Fun Facts

James first published his newspaper because a **smallpox** outbreak had shrunk his printing business, and he was looking for other ways to make a profit.

Actually, Ben knew who she was. Why? Because Silence Dogood and Ben Franklin were the same person! He had written the letters to show James what a good writer he was. Ben was so pleased he could barely keep the buttons from bursting off his shirt. But it was hard keeping the truth to himself.

Fun Facts

The *New-England Courant* published 14 letters from Mrs. Silence Dogood before her true identity was revealed.

Ben finally confessed everything to James. But was James impressed? Not at all. In fact, he was furious. How could Ben play such a trick? It was embarrassing for the *Courant*, and for James too.

A Chance to Grow

James wasn't only critical of Ben. He also complained about the government all the time. James and the government really did not get along. And city officials were getting as tired of him as he was of them.

Fun Facts

Colonial law allowed the governor to throw anyone in jail if he felt insulted by what the person had said.

Officials were so tired in fact, that at two different times they threw James in jail for a few weeks.

COMPETITION

When James was locked up, Ben ran the *Courant* by himself—which, to be honest, he didn't mind at all. And he did a good job. But James never thanked him for helping out. In truth, he was a bit jealous of his younger brother.

So things never got better between them. The brothers continued to fight, and not only with words alone. Sometimes, James even gave Ben a beating.

Fun Facts

Ben couldn't afford to buy many books, but he would borrow new ones overnight to read from bookseller apprentices and then return them in the morning.

Enough was enough. Ben was fed up. If James didn't appreciate him, he would go somewhere else. But where? His brother could keep him from finding printing work in Boston. It would be best to move away.

Fun Facts

Although Ben now knew the printing business, he could not officially call himself a printer in Boston because he had not finished his apprenticeship.

In 1723, New York wasn't as big a city as Boston. But it was a fresh place to start. And if things didn't work out there, Ben could go further south to Philadelphia.

Ben Makes His Escape

So Ben made plans to leave on a ship for New York. He boarded quietly at night, having already paid the captain to keep his **departure** a secret.

Someday, Ben was sure, his name would make people sit up and pay attention.

Fun Facts

The easiest and most comfortable way to travel from one city to another was by ship because roads or even paths barely existed.

And so 17-year-old Benjamin Franklin never looked back. His next adventure had arrived. And he was ready for it to start.

Fun Facts

Franklin ended up in Philadelphia where he built a profitable printing business before getting involved in politics.

Benjamin Franklin became famous for many things. He was a successful printer who also invented **bifocal** *eyeglasses and an indoor stove. He experimented with electricity and founded America's first post office. Perhaps most importantly, he was a statesman who helped lead the American colonies in their war of independence with Great Britain. He was also one of the people who signed the Declaration of Independence. Franklin lived until 1790, almost a year after George Washington became the first president of the new United States.*

GLOSSARY

apprentice
A person who works as an assistant to an established member of a trade, usually for a fixed number of years

bifocal
Divided into two parts that help a person to see things that are close and things that are far away

colonies
Areas of land under the control of a country that is far away from the land itself

departure
A time to leave one place to go to another

molds
Carved openings in wood or metal that hold liquids in specific shapes

petticoats
A kind of woman's clothing worn under a dress or skirt in addition to underwear

smallpox
A disease that causes a rash and a fever and often leads to death

vats
Large wooden barrels that hold liquids

vice
Bad behavior or habits

virtue
Good behavior or character

INDEX

COMPREHENSION QUESTIONS

Why was Ben so unhappy as a printer's apprentice?

Who did Ben pretend to be when he wrote letters to the *New-England Courant*?

Why was James Franklin thrown in jail?

ABOUT THE AUTHOR

Stephen Krensky is the award-winning author of more than 150 fiction and nonfiction books for children. He and his wife Joan live in Lexington, Massachusetts, and he happily spends as much time as possible with his grown children and not-so-grown grandchildren.

CRABTREE
Publishing Company

Written by: Stephen Krensky
Illustrations by: Bobbie Houser
Art direction and layout by: Bobbie Houser
Series Development: James Earley
Proofreader: Petrice Custance
Educational Consultant: Marie Lemke M.Ed.
Print Coordinator: Katherine Berti

Photographs: t = Top, c = Center, b = Bottom, l = Left, r = Right
Alamy: Smith Collection/Gado: p. 13 c; Chronicle: p. 15 t; SIPLEY/ClassicStock: p. 22 t; North Wind Picture Archives: p. 24 l; Getty: Kean Collection: p. 8 l; Historical: p. 26 b; Bettmann: p. 29 t; Granger: p. 7 c; Sarin Images: pp. 9 t, 11 r; pp. 12 c, 17 c, 19, 27 c; Shutterstock: hockey_mom: cover tl; Stocksnapper: cover bl, p. 29 b; Alex Staroseltsev: cover br; Eladora: p. 5 tc; Eroshka: p. 5 tlr; Thammanoon Khamchalee: p. 5 clr; shin88: p. 5 c; marekuliasz: p. 7 t; Pontus Edenberg: p. 7 b; Sergio Sergo: p. 8 r; Tartila: p. 9 b; fongbeerredhot: p. 11 l; DioGen: p. 12 r; Torsten Lorenz: p. 12 r; AKaiser: pp. 13 t, b, 27 b; Tomas Fabian: p. 15 b; snowyns: p. 16; New Design Illustrations: p. 17 tr; Kseniakrop: p. 17 br; Scisetti Alfio: p. 18 b; Pukhov K: p. 20; Martin Bergsma: p. 21; Aquir: p. 22 b; Digital Clipart: p. 23 tr; Reinhold Leitner: p. 23 bl; Jaromond: p. 24 r; ii-graphics: p. 25; igor malovic: p. 26 t

Library and Archives Canada Cataloguing in Publication

Available at the Library and Archives Canada

Library of Congress Cataloging-in-Publication Data

Available at the Library of Congress

Crabtree Publishing Company

www.crabtreebooks.com 1-800-387-7650

In Canada: We acknowledge the financial support of the Government of Canada through the Canada Book Fund for our publishing activities.

Published in the United States
Crabtree Publishing
347 Fifth Avenue
Suite 1402-145
New York, NY, 10016

Published in Canada
Crabtree Publishing
616 Welland Ave.
St. Catharines, ON
L2M 5V6

Printed in the U.S.A./072022/CG20220201